Pasta

Pasta

Published in 2008 by
Leonardo Publishing srl
Via Bordoni, 8 - 20124 MILAN, ITALY
www.leonardopublishing.com

Published originally under the title *Pasta*
© 2005 Food Editore srl
Via Mazzini, 6 - 43100 PARMA, ITALY
www.foodeditore.com

English Translation
Traduzioni Culinarie

Photographs
Alberto Rossi and Davide Di Prato

Recipes
Simone Rugiati and Licia Cagnoni

Thanks to
I Love My House (Barazzoni, Parma)

This 2008 edition printed exclusively for Barnes & Noble, Inc., by Food Editore srl.

ISBN-13: 978-88-6154-106-1

Printed and bound in China
10 9 8 7 6 5 4 3 2 1

The publisher reserves all rights to texts and illustrations in Italy and abroad. Rights to translation, electronic storage, and partial or total reproduction by any means (including microfilm or photocopies) in all countries are reserved by the publisher and may not be used by third parties without written consent of the publisher.

Pasta

Contents

Basic Techniques — 7

Short Pasta — 17

Long Pasta — 73

Special Recipes — 129

Useful Kitchen Tools — 138

Glossary — 140

Index — 142

Basic Techniques

PASTA: HISTORY AND LEGEND

The pleasure of coming home to a plate of pasta has been praised since the time of the Ancient Romans, cited by both Horace and the celebrated gourmet Apicius. In one of Boccaccio's stories in the fourteenth-century *Decameron*, ravioli and macaroni in capon broth roll down a mountain of grated cheese. These are just a few examples of the important role pasta has played in Italian cuisine through the ages.

The Romans apparently imported the tradition of *lagane*, a kind of thin pasta that was fried or boiled, from the Greeks. While this was a predecessor of our modern lasagne, it was the Arabs who first dried pasta and contributed to its spread throughout Italy. A ribbon-like pasta made from hard wheat, *trie*, first appeared in Palermo, while *maccheroni* was first documented in Genoa in 1279.

Pasta production in Naples came much later, but it was here that maccheroni became a food for popular consumption. Starting in the eighteenth century, the pasta could be bought from stalls and was eaten by hand on street corners. The classic marriage of pasta and tomatoes came only at the beginning of the nineteenth century, following widespread acceptance of the New World fruit as a food. Since then, pasta has been the star of Italian tables around the peninsula, as well one of the country's most successful

farfalle

tofe rigate

tagliatelle

caserecce

exports, with spaghetti Bolognese and macaroni and cheese now eaten around the world.

SHAPE AND TASTE

More than three hundred different kinds of pasta are produced in Italy. They are classified according to the flour used (hard or soft wheat) and their shape.

The different shapes don't only have an aesthetic effect, but actually have a profound impact on taste, even when exactly the same dough is used. The flavor changes with the pasta's form, which influences its ability to hold sauce. The shape is the key to the harmonious union of sauce and pasta, and each variation in the endless parade of forms offers a different sensation on the palate.

"Every sauce has its pasta and every pasta has its sauce," say Italians, reflecting a codification of rules regarding which sauce goes best with which pasta, based on centuries of tradition and a deep understanding of cooking pasta.

Dried pastas are divided into long and short shapes. The latter can be ridged or smooth. In general, the longer shapes pair well with thinner, more fluid fresh tomato sauces with fish or other seafood. For optimum results, thinner shapes can be drained while still undercooked, then finished in the pan with the sauce. This process allows the sauce to soak into the center of the pasta, resulting in a fuller and more intense flavor. Short pastas are best matched with thicker, heartier sauces, such as meat or vegetable ragùs. Shapes with cavities, such as cavatelli or gnocchi, can capture sauce ingredients, such as chickpeas or peas.

LONG PASTAS

The most common long pasta with a circular cross-section is undoubtedly spaghetti, the symbol of "Italianness" par excellence. References to pasta "in the guise of string" date back to 1244, but the regular production of spaghetti is far more recent. There are many variations, from the thin spaghettini, vermicelli, and capelli d'angelo (angel hair) to thick spaghettoni.

One unusual kind of spaghetti is known as spaghetti alla chitarra, an egg pasta with a square cross-section. Traditionally cut on a stringed, guitar-like box, its rough texture and thickness make it an

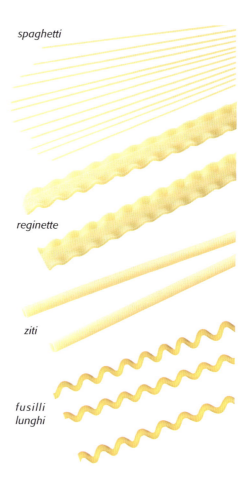

spaghetti

reginette

ziti

fusilli lunghi

excellent companion for meat- or fish-based sauces.

Linguine, which originated in the northwestern region called Liguria, is one of the best-known long pastas with a flat cross-section, which gives it a ribbon-like appearance. This type of pasta is normally paired with lighter sauces made with fish or shellfish, or different kinds of pesto.

While much shorter in the United States, where they're classified as a short pasta, ziti are actually long hollow tubes in Italy. Ziti are originally from the southern region of Campania, the capital of which is Naples. In the Neapolitan tradition, this pasta was served during wedding feasts, and in fact *zita* was the word used to refer to a young bride. Ziti are often broken to lengths of around 4 to 5 inches before cooking.

Another distinguished hollow shape in Italian cooking is bucatini. Originally from Lazio, a region in central Italy, this pasta looks like large spaghetti with a hole in the middle. It is the classic pasta for an Amatriciana sauce, which consists of tomatoes and *guanciale* (cured pig jowl) or pancetta, but it also works well with flavorful sauces that are quite thin and liquid, as these can reach the inner tube. Bucatini should not be broken before cooking. If you are unable to find bucatini for a recipe, you may substitute spaghetti.

SHORT PASTAS

The best-known short pasta is penne, which can be smooth or ridged (*lisce* or *rigate*, respectively). Mezze penne are half size, and pennette are even smaller. The name comes from *penna*, meaning feather or quill pen. Extremely versatile, this pasta shape holds almost any kind of sauce.

Fusilli are of southern origin, the Neapolitans being the first to come up with the idea of rolling spaghetti around a knitting needle to make a spiral. Naples was also the birthplace of hard-wheat gnocchi, which have a rounded form and central cavity that makes them able to hold the thickest, creamiest sauces, such as a classic Bolognese meat ragù.

The origins of rigatoni can be found in the city of Rome. These ridged tubes are perfect with rich meat and thick tomato sauces. They stand up well to long cooking times and hold sauces in a way that makes them ideal for timbales and baked pasta dishes.

Orecchiette, from Puglia (a region in southeastern Italy), translates to "little

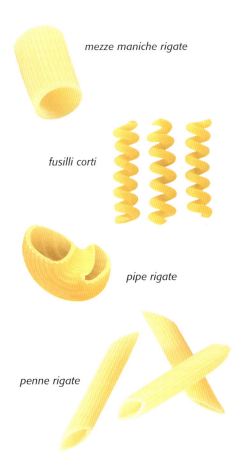

mezze maniche rigate

fusilli corti

pipe rigate

penne rigate

ears." These flat, indented shapes are usually served with thick, chunky sauces or sautéed bitter greens.

HOW TO RECOGNIZE GOOD PASTA

The most important characteristic of a good pasta is high quality raw materials. The kneading of the dough is also important, as is the technology used during production. The flour for pasta is ground from a mix of grains, with the best coming from Puglia in Italy, Arizona in the U.S., and Canada. Puglian grain has a good ability to maintain consistency during cooking. However, it has a pale color and is low in protein, so it is usually mixed with Arizona grain. Here are some guidelines on how to recognize good-quality pasta.

Appearance

Dried pasta should have a luminous, uniform aspect, without any cracks or stains. The color should be amber-yellow, but never too dark. An overly "toasted" color can indicate the presence of soft wheat, and above all is a sign that the pasta was dried at too-high temperatures, perhaps to save time. Pasta should snap cleanly, with a dry sound, when broken.

Cooking Water

The foam that rises to the surface when pasta is added to boiling water is not a sign of bad quality; rather, this effect is caused by air bubbles. However, the best pastas generally produce less foam. When pasta is drained, the water should still be clear. If it's cloudy, some of the pasta's starch has dissolved, meaning that a grain blend of poor quality was used for the flour.

THE SECRETS OF COOKING

The key to making a good pasta dish is not just in buying high-quality pasta made with the best ingredients and techniques, but also in following some simple rules of cooking:

1. Use at least 4 cups (1 quart) of water for every 3½ ounces of pasta (Italians usually estimate about 3 to 3½ ounces of pasta per person). Also, use a large, high-sided pot so that the temperature of the water remains constant, which prevents the pasta from sticking together.

2. Once the water reaches a full boil (never before), add about 1 teaspoon of sea salt for every 3½ ounces of pasta, and let the salt dissolve.

3. When the water has returned to a boil, add the pasta. Because adding the pasta leads to a decrease in water temperature, it is advisable to raise the heat at this point in order to maintain a boil. Long pasta should be spread out like a fan and never broken, while short pasta should be sprinkled in to avoid clumping together at the bottom of the pot. Pasta nests should be immersed in water and then immediately unraveled with the help of a large fork or a wooden spoon.

4. Gently stir the pasta, frequently at the beginning to stop it from sticking, and then every so often during the rest of the cooking time.

5. Drain the pasta when it is al dente ("to the tooth"), meaning it gives just a little resistance when bitten into. While every pasta shape has its own cooking time, the best way to test doneness is to taste it. A sample piece of pasta can also be broken: If it is still white in the center, then it needs to cook for about 1 more minute. When it's ready, drain the pasta, reserving a little of the cooking water in case the sauce needs to be thinned.

6. Transfer the drained pasta to a serving bowl and toss with the sauce so that it is uniformly absorbed. If the recipe calls for the cooked pasta to be sautéed in a pan, drain it a minute before it is done and finish cooking in the sauce, over high heat.

7. Do not rinse the pasta under cold water because it will lose the layer of starch that helps the sauce adhere. The only exceptions occur with regard to cold pastas and some buttery sauces.

BASIC SAUCES

Sauces made with tomatoes, either on their own or with other ingredients, are

undoubtedly the most common pairings for pasta, regardless of the shape of the pasta. It is hard to imagine today that for more than five hundred years pasta was consumed without this simple and tasty companion. The first culinary use of the tomato in Italy seems to have occurred in Naples. Toward the end of the eighteenth century, this fruit's good conservation qualities were discovered, and soon thereafter, the tomato began to appear in cookbooks, marking its official entry into the Italian diet. Since that time, it has become a staple. A wide range of preserved tomato products are available on the market, from canned whole plum tomatoes to tomato puree. The following recipes call for either canned whole peeled plum tomatoes, known as *pelati* in Italian, or canned crushed tomatoes. During the summer, fresh tomatoes can be used when they are at the peak of ripeness; they should be blanched and peeled for a smooth sauce.

Here are some recipes for tomato-based sauces, with some flavorful variations.

through a food mill, then add to the pan and gently cook for around 10 minutes, stirring often. Add the basil leaves and a pinch of salt at the end.

Classic Tomato Sauce

Serves 4

2 to 3 tablespoons extra-virgin olive oil
½ carrot, peeled and minced
1 celery stalk, fibers removed, minced
½ white onion, minced
2 cups (13 ounces) canned peeled plum tomatoes, in their juice
5 basil leaves
1 pinch salt

Heat the oil in a saucepan and sauté the carrot, celery, and onion for 3 to 4 minutes over low heat. Crush the tomatoes with a spoon or pass them

Chef's Advice

Adding a pinch of sugar to the tomatoes while cooking helps cut their acidity. The canned peeled plum tomatoes can also be replaced by canned crushed tomatoes.

The carrot, celery, and onion can be minced in a food processor, but pulse so as not to overheat the vegetables.

Spicy Tomato Sauce

Serves 4

1 garlic clove
½ red chili pepper (dried or fresh)
3 tablespoons extra-virgin olive oil

1 cup (6½ ounces) canned
   crushed tomatoes
salt and pepper

Peel the garlic clove and cut it in half. Discard the inner green shoot and mince the rest. Remove the seeds from the chili pepper and crumble it or finely mince. Heat the oil in a saucepan with the garlic and chili pepper. Just before the garlic browns, add the tomatoes and cook over medium heat for 10 minutes, adding a little water halfway through and seasoning with pinches of salt and pepper to taste.

Chef's Advice
The amount of garlic and chili pepper can be varied according to taste. However, the chili seeds should always be removed, as they are strong and not very aromatic. If you don't like a lot of garlic, leave the clove whole and lightly smash it, then brown briefly in the oil and remove before adding the tomatoes. In the summer, the canned crushed tomatoes can be replaced by ripe fresh tomatoes that are blanched, peeled, seeded, and chopped.

The choice between a sweeter or spicier sauce is a question of taste. In any case, make sure not to use too much sauce with the pasta, or you run the risk of completely masking the basic flavor of the pasta.

All'Amatriciana Variation
Brown a thinly sliced white onion in a frying pan with 3 tablespoons extra-virgin olive oil, then add about 3½ ounces pancetta, cut into matchstick-shaped pieces. As soon as the fat starts to render, add 1 cup (6½ ounces) canned crushed tomatoes and cook for about 10 minutes.

Season generously with salt and pepper.

The original recipe from the town of Amatrice, located in Lazio, calls for pasta tossed with *guanciale* (cured pig jowl) browned in oil, then sprinkled with pepper and grated Pecorino Romano cheese.

Mediterranean Variation
Blanch 3 ripe San Marzano (or plum) tomatoes for 30 seconds, then immerse in cold water. Peel, remove the seeds, and chop. Sauté 1 smashed garlic clove (or ½ minced clove) in 3 tablespoons extra-virgin olive oil with 2 teaspoons pine nuts and 2 anchovy fillets in oil. Add 1 cup (6½ ounces) canned crushed tomatoes, 5 rinsed capers, and 15 olives. Continue cooking, adding a little of the reserved pasta water. Stir in basil, salt, and pepper to taste.

To ease peeling, cut an X in the base of the tomatoes before blanching.

Spiced Vegetable Variation

Sauté 1 minced spring onion in a frying pan with 3 tablespoons extra-virgin olive oil. Add ½ diced red bell pepper and sauté for 5 minutes. Remove the seeds from and dice ½ eggplant and 2 zucchini, and add to pan, along with ¾ cup (3½ ounces) peas. Separately, heat ¾ cup (5½ ounces) canned crushed tomatoes, then add to the vegetables with 1 teaspoon mixed ground spices (cumin, nutmeg, coriander). Cook for about 10 minutes. Add salt and pepper to taste.

Alla Norma Variation

Thinly slice 1 eggplant, sprinkle with salt, and leave in a colander for at least 30 minutes. Sauté 1 smashed garlic clove in a frying pan with 2 tablespoons extra-virgin olive oil. Add 3 chopped tomatoes to the pan. Cook for 2 minutes, then add 6 basil leaves basil, chopped. Remove from heat and set aside. Rinse the eggplant, pat dry, and chop, then fry in hot sunflower oil. Drain on paper towels, adding the eggplant to the tomatoes together with cooked pasta (spaghetti or penne). Sprinkle with 2 tablespoons grated ricotta salata and stir just before serving.

Pesto

Pesto is another historic sauce. While it's originally from Liguria, infinite variations exist.

Genoese Pesto

Serves 6

35 to 40 fresh basil leaves
coarse salt
4 to 5 garlic cloves
2 tablespoons grated Pecorino Sardo cheese
2 tablespoons grated Parmesan cheese
6 tablespoons extra-virgin olive oil

Crush the basil, salt, and garlic with a mortar and pestle until mashed in a paste. Add the grated cheeses and continue to work the mixture with a wooden spatula, scraping it off the sides. When the paste is uniform, add the oil, pouring in a thin stream and stirring to obtain a smooth cream.

Variations

For an eastern Ligurian pesto, add fresh or toasted pine nuts and reduce the amount of garlic. For a lighter, garlic-free version, pound about 25 fresh basil leaves, 1 scant tablespoon pine nuts, 1 walnut, 5 tablespoons mild extra-virgin olive oil, 1 tablespoon grated Parmesan, and a pinch of salt until smooth and creamy.

Chef's Advice

It's best to use a wooden or stone mortar, because metal can alter the flavor of basil. When using a food processor, pulse the basil so it doesn't heat up and discolor.

Ligurian basil will impart a distinctive flavor and should be used whenever possible. Proportions of the different ingredients change from recipe to recipe, but one common rule recommends 5 basil leaves for every garlic clove.

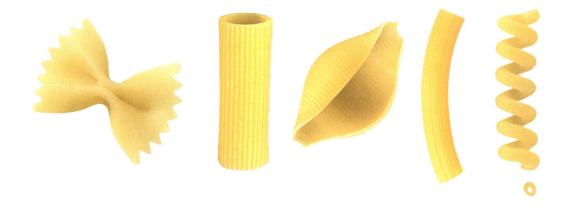

Short Pasta

Farfalle, rigatoni, fusilli–discover the world of short pasta, along with new and original sauces. The following pages present quick and easy recipes, featuring healthy and natural ingredients. From meat to fish, cheese to vegetables, there are many choices to inspire the imagination and whet the appetite.

Egg Fusilli with Vegetables

Serves 4

½ eggplant, seeded and cut into strips
salt
3 small artichokes
juice of 1 lemon
¼ cup extra-virgin olive oil
2 garlic cloves, smashed
1 small leek, thinly sliced
1 dried red chili pepper
½ cup hot vegetable broth
1 tomato, diced or cut into thin wedges
parsley, minced
14 ounces dried egg fusilli

Preparation time 40 minutes
Cooking time 15 minutes
Level easy
Wine young, medium-bodied white with bouquet of yellow fruits, such as Friuli Sauvignon Blanc

Place the eggplant in a colander. Sprinkle with salt, and let sit at least 30 minutes.

Meanwhile, trim the artichokes by cutting off the stem, removing the hard outer leaves, and cutting off the leaf tips. Cut each artichoke in half, and scoop out and discard the choke. Slice into thin pieces, then let soak in a bowl of cold water with lemon juice.

Heat the olive oil in a frying pan with the garlic cloves, leek, and chili pepper. Let cook over low heat for 5 minutes.

Drain and dry the eggplant, and add to the pan. Drain the artichokes and add to the pan as well. Cook for 6 to 7 minutes, adding a little hot broth, and stirring frequently.

Add the tomato, salt to taste, and sprinkle with parsley. Cook the pasta in a large pot of salted boiling water until al dente. Drain, add to the pan with the sauce, and toss to coat. Serve hot.

Cavatappi with Artichokes, Shellfish, and Tomatoes

Serves 4

15 cherry tomatoes, halved
salt and pepper
5 medium langoustines
5 large shrimp
5 tablespoons extra-virgin olive oil
5 tablespoons chopped shallot
1 small carrot, chopped
1 celery stalk, chopped
1 parsley sprig
2 garlic cloves, 1 halved and 1 smashed
1 bunch turnip tops or broccoli rabe, trimmed
2 violet or purple artichokes
½ red chili pepper, seeded
thyme
1 tablespoon crab meat
7 ounces cavatappi

Preparation time 20 minutes
Cooking time 1 hour 20 minutes
Level easy
Wine white with well-structured body and evolved bouquet, such as Sicily Chardonnay Barrique

Place the cherry tomatoes on a baking sheet, sprinkle with salt, and let them dry in the oven, set on the lowest possible setting, for 1 hour.
　Shell the langoustines and shrimp, reserving the shells and heads. Dice the meat, place in a container, cover with plastic wrap, and store in the refrigerator.
　Heat 3 tablespoons olive oil and sauté the shallot, carrot, and celery. Add the shells and heads and sauté over high heat. Cover with very cold water, add the parsley, and cook for 30 minutes. Strain the broth, then continue cooking to reduce to a third of the original volume.
　Heat 2 tablespoons olive oil and the halved garlic in a frying pan and sauté the turnip tops. Continue cooking until tender, adding a little water if necessary, then remove and discard the garlic.
　Trim the artichokes, leaving only the heart. Dice and sauté in a frying pan with the smashed garlic and the chili pepper. Add the shrimp and langoustines, then the crab. Add the reduced broth and continue cooking until the shellfish are cooked through.
　Cook the pasta in a large pot of salted boiling water until al dente. Drain and add to the pan with the sauce. Continue cooking to reduce and thicken the sauce, then season with salt and pepper, to taste. Stir in the cherry tomatoes.
　Serve the pasta over a bed of sautéed turnip tops.

Saffron Farfalle with Asparagus

SAFFRON
Saffron is made from the dried stigmas of the saffron crocus flower, which blooms in autumn for just two weeks. The spice is very expensive as it takes 150,000 flowers to make approximately 2 pounds of saffron. If the saffron does not immediately dissolve when immersed in water, it is impure or old.

Serves 4

10 asparagus spears
3 tablespoons extra-virgin olive oil
1 shallot, minced
½ cup vegetable broth
salt
1 pinch saffron
12½ ounces farfalle
2 hardboiled eggs, yolks only
parsley, minced

Preparation time 15 minutes
Cooking time 25 minutes
Level easy
Wine young white with medium body and grassy notes, such as Alto Adige Pinot Bianco

Peel the bottoms of the asparagus spears and slice the spears into rounds.
  Heat the olive oil in a saucepan and sauté the shallot. Add the asparagus and broth and cook over low heat for 5 minutes.
  Bring a large pot of water to a boil and salt. Add the saffron, let dissolve, then cook the farfalle in the saffron water until al dente. Drain, rinse with cold water, transfer to the saucepan, and toss with the asparagus over high heat. Crumble the egg yolks, stir in with the pasta and asparagus, and sprinkle with parsley.

Note When sauteeing the asparagus, leave the spears very al dente, so that when the pasta is tossed with the sauce and the spears reheat, they don't get overcooked. Stir in the crumbled egg yolk just before serving to make the sauce creamy.

Giant Paccheri with Fish

Serves 4

¾ pound grouper
1 garlic clove, minced
½ red chili pepper, minced
2 tablespoons extra-virgin olive oil
½ cup white wine
10 cherry tomatoes, quartered
salt and white pepper
parsley, minced
11½ ounces giant paccheri (or rigatoni)

Preparation time 20 minutes
Cooking time 25 minutes
Level medium
Wine white with good body and long persistence,
such as Campania Greco di Tufo

If using a whole fish, clean and gut the fish, and wash well. Fillet the fish, remove the bones from the fillets with kitchen tweezers, and set aside. Reserve the fish scraps.

Sauté the garlic and chili pepper in the olive oil in a frying pan. Add the fish scraps and sauté over high heat to extract all the flavor. Pour in the wine and cook, covered, for 7 to 8 minutes.

Dice the fillets.

Add the tomatoes to the pan and let simmer slowly. Remove the fish scraps, then add the diced fillets. Season with salt and pepper and cook for 3 minutes. Add the minced parsley.

Cook the pasta in a large pot of salted boiling water until al dente. Drain and toss in the pan with the fish and tomatoes.

Note If you unable to find paccheri or giant paccheri for this recipe, you may substitute rigatoni.

Penne with Green-Bean Pesto and Pine Nuts

Serves 4

3 cups (12½ ounces) green beans, trimmed
4 tablespoons extra-virgin olive oil
1 small onion, minced
1 garlic clove, smashed
salt and pepper
6 basil leaves
12½ ounces smooth penne
2½ tablespoons toasted pine nuts

Preparation time 25 minutes
Cooking time 10 minutes
Level easy
Wine light white with body and herbaceous notes, such as Liguria Vermentino

Boil the green beans in salted water for about 10 minutes. Drain, reserving the cooking water and keeping it warm.
　Heat the oil and sauté the onion and garlic until soft. Add the green beans (reserving a few for garnish), ½ cup of the cooking water, and a pinch of salt. Cook for another 10 to 15 minutes, then remove from the heat and let cool.
　Puree the cooled beans with the basil and a little of the cooking water to obtain a smooth sauce. Season with salt and pepper and keep warm.
　Bring the green-bean cooking water back to a boil and cook the penne until al dente. Drain and toss with the pesto. Drizzle with oil and sprinkle with pepper, reserved green beans, and pine nuts, then serve.

Variation You can give this dish additional flavor by adding grated aged ricotta or shavings of peppered pecorino just before serving. For a lighter flavor, add a few mint leaves to the pesto and garnish the pasta with some crumbled feta cheese.

Paccheri with Langoustines and Eggplant

Serves 4

15 small langoustines or jumbo shrimp
3 tablespoons extra-virgin olive oil
1 ¼ cups minced celery, carrot and onion
½ cup white wine
salt
1 small eggplant, seeded and diced (photo 1)
sunflower oil
14 ounces paccheri (or rigatoni)
1 shallot, minced
½ dried red chili pepper
10 cherry tomatoes, chopped
parsley, minced

Preparation time 20 minutes
Cooking time 1 hour 30 minutes
Level medium
Wine well-structured, very persistent white, such as Tuscany Chardonnay Barrique

Using kitchen scissors, cut the langoustine tails open and extract the tail meat, keeping it intact. Reserve the shells and heads.

Heat 1 tablespoon extra-virgin olive oil and sauté the minced celery, carrot, and onion. Add the shells, heads, and wine. Reduce and cover with cold water. Simmer for 1 hour 30 minutes. Pass through a food mill and season with salt.

Meanwhile, fry the eggplant in the sunflower oil, then drain on paper towels.

Cook the pasta in a large pot of salted boiling water until al dente.

Heat the remaining olive oil and sauté the shallot and chili pepper. Add the tomatoes and sauté over high heat briefly. Add the langoustines and the eggplant (photo 2). Sprinkle with parsley and pour in some langoustine broth. Lower the heat and simmer. When the pasta is al dente, drain and add to the pan with the sauce (photo 3). Finish cooking in the pan, adding more broth if necessary.

Note If you are unable to find paccheri for this recipe, you may substitute rigatoni.

Strozzapreti with Calabrian Pesto

Serves 4

salt
1 bunch of basil
2 garlic cloves
2 tablespoons pine nuts
10 pitted black olives
2 tablespoons capers
10 sun-dried tomatoes
2 tablespoons extra-virgin olive oil
1⅓ cups (7 ounces) cherry tomatoes, diced
10½ ounces fresh strozzapreti

Preparation time 20 minutes
Cooking time 20 minutes
Level easy
Wine well-structured white with intense bouquet, such as Campania Fiano di Avellino

Bring a large pot of salted water to a boil.

Meanwhile mince together the basil, garlic, pine nuts, olives, capers, and sun-dried tomatoes, using a knife or a food processor.

Heat the oil in a nonstick frying pan and sauté the cherry tomatoes for 1 minute. Add the basil mixture and sauté over high heat briefly.

Cook the strozzapreti in the boiling water until al dente, then drain and toss in the frying pan with the sauce. Serve hot.

Note The name *strozzapreti* means "priest-chokers." According to legend, women would prepare this pasta for the local priest, while their husbands, clearly less devout, hoped that the priest would choke while stuffing himself with the delicacy.

Radiatori with Zucchini, Anchovies, and Arugula

ANCHOVIES

The anchovy is a small, oily fish–a great delicacy that is rich in protein and can be preserved or eaten fresh. In Italy, anchovy fishing begins in May–the best month because the fish are leaner at that time–and continues until December.

Serves 4

20 fresh anchovies
2 tablespoons extra-virgin olive oil
1 garlic clove, minced
½ dried red chili pepper
8 baby zucchini, quartered lengthways
1 tomato, seeded and chopped
½ bunch broad-leaved arugula, finely chopped
salt and white pepper
1 oregano sprig, minced
13½ ounces dried egg radiatori (or rotini)

Preparation time 15 minutes
Cooking time 15 minutes
Level easy
Wine medium-bodied white, such as Alto Adige Pinot Bianco

Wash the anchovies and open each like a book, removing the head and backbone.

Heat the oil in a frying pan with the garlic and chili pepper. Add the zucchini and sauté for 2 minutes. Add the anchovies and sauté briefly, then add the tomato and arugula. Season with white pepper and the oregano.

Cook the pasta in a large pot of salted boiling water until al dente. While the pasta is cooking, add a few spoonfuls of the cooking water to the sauce.

Drain the pasta and toss with the sauce in the pan, then serve.

Variation If desired, you can add a handful of toasted pine nuts or 2 minced sun-dried tomatoes to the sauce.

Shells with Porcini and Squash Blossoms

Serves 4

3 tablespoons extra-virgin olive oil
2 shallots, minced
1 large fresh porcini mushroom (about 5½ ounces), chopped
1⅓ cups (3½ ounces) chopped white mushrooms
salt and pepper
8 squash blossoms, finely chopped
½ cup vegetable broth
1 tablespoon heavy cream
1 tablespoon cornstarch
11 ounces large pasta shells
parsley, minced

Preparation time 20 minutes
Cooking time 30 minutes
Level easy
Wine young, medium-bodied, fresh, light rosé,
such as Bardolino Chiaretto

Heat 2 tablespoons of the olive oil in a frying pan and add ½ of the minced shallots. Sauté over low heat until transluscent and tender, then add the mushrooms. Season with salt and pepper and sauté for 10 minutes.

Meanwhile, heat the remaining olive oil in a small saucepan and add the remainder of the minced shallots. When soft, add the squash blossoms. Pour in the broth and cook for 5 minutes. Add the cream and whisk in the cornstarch to thicken the sauce.

Cook the pasta in a large pot of salted boiling water until al dente. Drain, then fill the shells with the mushrooms. Sprinkle with parsley and serve on top of the squash blossom sauce.

Note The mushrooms in this sauce are cooked for a fairly long time, so if out of season, they could be replaced by mixed frozen mushrooms. After cooking, puree them into a smooth sauce before serving.

Cold Tortiglioni with Peas and Roasted Peppers

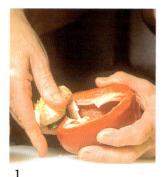

Serves 4

1 red bell pepper
2 tablespoons extra-virgin olive oil
1 shallot, minced
½ cup vegetable broth
1 cup (4 ounces) spring peas
2 carrots, diced (photo 2)
3 tablespoons heavy cream
2 tablespoons lemon thyme leaves, chopped
salt and pepper
14 ounces tortiglioni (or rigatoni)

Preparation time 20 minutes
Cooking time 10 minutes
Level easy
Wine white with unstructured body and evolved bouquet, such as Campania Falanghina

Preheat the oven to 475°F.
 Cut the pepper in half, core, and seed (photo 1). Wash under running water, dry well, then brush lightly with about 1 tablespoon olive oil and cut into thick strips. Place on a baking sheet and roast in the oven for 10 minutes. Remove from oven, place in a plastic bag, and let sit for 15 minutes to steam. Peel and set aside.
 Heat 1 tablespoon olive oil and sauté the shallot. Add the vegetable broth. Add the peas (photo 3) and carrots. Cook for 10 minutes, then remove from the heat and let cool.
 Add the peppers, cream, and thyme to the peas and carrots, and season with salt and pepper to taste.
 Cook the pasta in a large pot of salted boiling water until al dente. Drain and cool under cold running water. Toss with the vegetables, then let sit for 20 minutes before serving.

Shells with Peas and Carrots

Serves 4

2 tablespoons butter
1 shallot, minced
4 cups (32 ounces) hot vegetable broth
1 ½ cups (7 ounces) peas
salt and pepper
1 teaspoon fresh goat cheese
3 tablespoons extra-virgin olive oil
12 ½ ounces medium shells
2 carrots, diced
1 tablespoon grated Parmesan

Preparation time 10 minutes
Cooking time 20 minutes
Level easy
Wine young, light white with body and grassy bouquet, such as Veneto Lugana

Melt the butter in a saucepan and sauté the shallot until soft, adding a little broth if necessary. Add the peas and cook for 5 minutes, seasoning with salt and pepper. Cover with hot broth and cook until peas are tender.

Puree the peas with the goat cheese and 2 tablespoons olive oil, using an immersion blender or a food processor. Adjust salt and pepper to taste.

Cook the pasta in a large pot of salted boiling water until al dente.

Meanwhile heat 1 tablespoon olive oil in a frying pan and sauté the carrots.

Drain the pasta and mix with the pea puree. Stir the Parmesan into the pasta and serve with the sautéed carrots.

Variation For a richer dish, top individual servings of the pasta with shavings of Pecorino Romano and freshly ground black pepper. The carrots can be replaced with diced sun-dried tomato, sautéed briefly with a little oil and water.

Spicy Penne

Serves 4

4 tablespoons extra-virgin olive oil
1 small onion, diced
1 garlic clove
7 ounces pork sausage meat, chopped
dried red chili peppers
2 2/3 cups (1 pound) canned whole tomatoes, deseeded and chopped
salt
10 1/2 ounces ridged penne
4 1/2 ounces fresh mozzarella, chopped
3 tablespoons grated Parmesan
8 basil leaves

Preparation time 10 minutes
Cooking time 35 minutes
Level easy
Wine well-structured white with good acidity,
such as Campania Greco di Tufo

Heat the olive oil in a large frying pan. Add the onion and the whole garlic clove. Add the sausage meat to the pan and sauté briefly. Crumble over as many dried chile peppers as desired and add the tomatoes. Season to taste with salt and cook for 20 minutes.

Bring a large pot of salted water to a boil and add the penne. Cook until al dente, drain and add to the pan with the sauce. Stir to coat the pasta and transfer half the pasta to a warmed serving bowl. Add half the mozzarella, Parmesan cheese, and basil. Add the remaining pasta and top with the remaining mozzarella, Parmesan cheese, and basil. Let sit for few minutes until the mozzarella melts, then serve immediately.

Note This hearty pasta sauce pairs well with large shell-shaped pasta (conchiglioni rigati). For an elegant presentation, serve the pasta in small ramekins.

Anelli with Clams, Potatoes, and Tomatoes

Serves 4

14 ounces littleneck clams
salt
¼ cup extra-virgin olive oil
1 garlic clove, minced
½ red chili pepper, minced
2 small yellow-fleshed potatoes, peeled and diced
10 cherry tomatoes, quartered
1 teaspoon minced parsley
10½ ounces anelli (or rigatoni)

Preparation time 15 minutes
Cooking time 15 minutes
Level easy
Wine medium-bodied, fresh white with herbaceous notes, such as Alto Adige Sauvignon

Wash the clams well under cold running water, brushing with a stiff brush. Let soak in cold, salted water for at least 1 hour to purge any sand.

Heat the olive oil in a frying pan and gently sauté the garlic with the chili pepper until soft. Add the potatoes and continue cooking over medium heat, adding a little hot water. After 5 minutes, add the clams and raise the heat. Cover and cook until the clams open. Add the tomatoes. Continue cooking until the potatoes are tender. Season lightly with salt, and sprinkle with parsley.

Cook the pasta in a large pot of salted boiling water until al dente. Drain and add to the sauce. Sauté briefly over high heat, then serve.

Variation This recipe can be modified by adding 3 tablespoons pesto to the sauce when you add the pasta. Prepare a pesto without garlic or Parmesan by pureeing 1 bunch basil, 1 teaspoon pine nuts, and 3 to 4 walnut halves with extra-virgin olive oil. If you are unable to find anelli for this recipe, you may substitute rigatoni.

Ligurian-Style Rice Sedanini

Serves 4

4 tablespoons extra-virgin olive oil
1 garlic clove, peeled and smashed
1 tablespoon toasted pine nuts
15 cured black olives, pitted
10 cherry tomatoes, halved
8 basil leaves, minced
salt and pepper
12½ ounces rice sedanini (or penne)
1 tablespoon minced chives
1 carrot, peeled and grated

Preparation time 10 minutes
Cooking time 10 minutes
Level easy
Wine medium-bodied, intense and persistent,
such as white Liguria Pigato

Heat the olive oil and sauté the garlic until golden. Add the pine nuts, olives, tomatoes, and basil. Salt to taste and add a little hot water. Cook for 5 minutes, then adjust salt and pepper.

Cook the pasta in a large pot of salted boiling water until al dente. Drain and toss in the pan with the sauce. Stir in the chives and divide between serving plates.

Top with grated carrot and serve.

Note Even people with gluten intolerances do not have to give up pasta. Pastas made with rice flour or corn make excellent alternatives to wheat. Rice pasta is also more digestible and lower in calories than traditional pasta.

Paccheri with Three Peppers in White Sauce

Serves 4

Filling
3 tablespoons extra-virgin olive oil
1 garlic clove, smashed
½ yellow bell pepper, finely diced
½ red bell pepper, finely diced
½ green bell pepper, finely diced
9 ounces sheep's milk ricotta (or cow's milk ricotta that has been drained overnight)
6 sun-dried tomatoes, 3 minced and 3 julienned
3 tablespoons grated Pecorino Romano cheese
salt and pepper
1 bunch chives, blanched

Sauce
1 cup milk
3 garlic cloves
2 tablespoons butter
2½ tablespoons cornstarch
hot vegetable broth

Pasta
24 paccheri (or rigatoni)

Garnish
3 tablespoons extra-virgin olive oil
1 leek, julienned
3 sun-dried tomatoes, julienned

Preparation time 25 minutes
Cooking time 35 minutes
Level medium
Wine well-structured white with very persistent grassy notes, such as Trentino Müller Thurgau

Preheat the oven to 400°F.

Heat a little of the olive oil in a frying pan with the smashed garlic. Sauté the peppers separately, one color at a time, then reserve, keeping the colors separate.

To prepare the sauce, bring the milk to a boil with the 3 garlic cloves and keep warm.

Melt the butter, and whisk in the cornstarch, then add the hot milk, discarding the garlic. Whisk until thickened, then add enough hot broth to make a fluid sauce.

Cook the pasta in a large pot of salted boiling water until al dente, drain, and cool. Meanwhile beat the ricotta with the minced sun-dried tomatoes, pecorino, and the remaining olive oil designated for the filling. Season with salt and pepper.

Stuff the cooled pasta with the ricotta mixture and place each upright on a baking sheet in a group of 6. Tie each cluster with the blanched chives and top with sautéed pepper. Bake for 12 minutes.

Heat 3 tablespoons olive oil and fry the julienned leek until golden and crispy.

Serve the pasta over the white sauce and top with the julienned sun-dried tomatoes and fried leek.

Pasta with Radish Sprouts, Broccoli, and Artichokes

Serves 4

12½ ounces corn fusilli
¼ cup extra-virgin olive oil
4 small artichokes
1 garlic clove
1 head broccoli, cut into florets
2 ounces Pecorino Romano, shaved
1 tablespoon ground thyme
1 teaspoon sesame seeds
1½ cup radish sprouts
salt and pepper

Preparation time 20 minutes
Cooking time 20 minutes
Level easy
Wine young, medium-bodied, fresh and fragrant white,
such as Veneto Gambellara

Cook the pasta in a large pot of salted boiling water until al dente. Drain and rinse under running water, then place in a large salad bowl. Toss with 2 tablespoons olive oil. Trim the artichokes, removing and discarding the hard outer leaves and the inner choke. Cut the trimmed artichokes into thin slices.

Heat 1 tablespoon olive oil and sauté the garlic until golden. Add the artichokes and sauté for 5 minutes over high heat.

Blanch the broccoli florets for a few minutes, then drain and add to the pasta together with the artichokes, Pecorino Romano shavings, thyme, sesame seeds, and radish sprouts. Season with salt and pepper and drizzle with a little oil.

Note If you have leftover pasta, you can make pan-fried croquettes. Coarsely chop the pasta and mix with an egg. Season the mixture with minced herbs, if desired; then cook a small amount at a time in a nonstick frying pan with extra-virgin olive oil to form the croquettes. The mixture can also be shaped into balls, coated with breadcrumbs, and fried. Serve with mixed vegetables or a salad.

Campanelle with Peppers and Escarole

Serves 4

½ head escarole, shredded
3 tablespoons extra-virgin olive oil
1 garlic clove, smashed
salt and pepper
12 pitted Gaeta or Kalamata olives
½ red bell pepper, finely diced
2 tablespoons ground thyme
14 ounces dried egg campanelle
grated Pecorino Romano or aged ricotta salata

BLACK OLIVES
The color of olives does not come from the variety, but from ripeness. When underripe, olives are green; they later reach a deep black-violet color when fully ripe. One of the best-known Italian olive varieties is Gaeta, which has a slightly bitter flavor and a gentle acidity.

Preparation time 15 minutes
Cooking time 20 minutes
Level easy
Wine full-bodied white with evolved bouquet of ripe fruit, such as Sicily Chardonnay Barrique

Soak the escarole in a bowl of cold water.

Heat 2 tablespoons olive oil and sauté the garlic until golden. Drain the escarole and add to the pan. Stir well, season with salt, and cook, covered, for 5 minutes. Add the olives and a little water, cover again, and cook until the escarole is tender and transparent.

Heat 1 tablespoon olive oil in a frying pan and sauté the red pepper with the thyme until soft.

Cook the pasta in a large pot of salted boiling water until al dente. Drain and add to the pan with the peppers. Add the escarole, then season with black pepper to taste. Stir well. Serve the pasta with grated Pecorino Romano or aged ricotta salata.

Corn Fusilli with Shiitake and Porcini Mushrooms

Serves 4

2 dried shiitake mushrooms
2 fresh porcini mushrooms
3 tablespoons extra-virgin olive oil
1 garlic clove, smashed
½ dried red chili pepper, seeded and crumbled
1 mint sprig
1 tablespoon parsley, minced
½ cup vegetable broth
salt
14 ounces corn fusilli

Preparation time 10 minutes
Cooking time 15 minutes
Level easy
Wine young, light-bodied, fresh red with notes of red fruits,
such as Friuli Merlot

Soak the dried shiitake mushrooms in water for several hours, with a plate on top to keep them immersed.

Detach and reserve the stalks of the shiitakes and the porcini, and clean the porcini well with a damp paper towel. Dice the stalks and slice the caps of the mushrooms.

Heat the olive oil in a frying pan and sauté the garlic with the chili pepper until golden. Add the mushroom stalks and caps, and sauté together with the mint and parsley. After 5 minutes add a little vegetable broth.

Cook the fusilli in a large pot of salted boiling water until al dente. Drain and toss with the mushrooms in the frying pan.

Anelli with Eggplant and Tomatoes

Serves 4

1 small, long eggplant, cut into wedges
salt and pepper
3 tablespoons extra-virgin olive oil
1 shallot, minced
½ red chili pepper, seeded and minced
2 tablespoons thyme leaves
15 cherry tomatoes, quartered and seeded
14 ounces anelli (or rigatoni)
7 ounces cow's-milk mozzarella, diced

EGGPLANT
Eggplant is a typical Mediterranean vegetable (technically, a fruit), harvested during the summer. Longer varieties, such as the Violetta di Napoli, have a spicier flavor than round ones, such as the Violetta di Firenze, or oval ones such as Black Beauty, which has a very dark purple hue.

Preparation time 15 minutes
Cooking time 10 minutes
Level easy
Wine young, medium-bodied white with very persistent bouquet, such as Tuscany Chardonnay

Salt the eggplant wedges and leave in a colander for at least 30 minutes.
Drain the eggplant and remove the central, seedy part. Dice the rest.
Heat the olive oil and sauté the shallot with the chili pepper until soft. Add the eggplant and sauté over high heat for 5 minutes. Add the thyme leaves and tomatoes. Season lightly with salt and pepper and cook for another 5 minutes.
Meanwhile cook the pasta in a large pot of salted boiling water until al dente. Drain, reserving a bit of the cooking water, and add the pasta to the pan with the eggplant and tomatoes. Add a little of the cooking water if necessary to thin the sauce. Toss to coat, then stir in the mozzarella.

Note Add extra color and flavor to this dish by stirring in a tablespoon of basil pesto (see page 14) just before serving. If you are unable to find anelli for this recipe, you may substitute rigatoni.

Rotelle with Peppers, Ricotta, and Arugula

Serves 4

½ red bell pepper
½ yellow bell pepper
1 bunch arugula
10½ ounces rotelle (wheel-shaped pasta)
2 ounces aged ricotta salata, shaved
2 tablespoons extra-virgin olive oil
salt and pepper

Preparation time 20 minutes
Cooking time 15 minutes
Level easy
Wine young, light-bodied white with herbaceous notes,
such as Alto Adige Pinot Bianco

Roast the peppers over an open flame until blackened. Transfer to a plastic bag, close, and let steam for at least 10 to 15 minutes.
  Meanwhile soak the arugula in cold water to make it crisp.
  Cook the pasta in a large pot of salted boiling water until al dente. Drain and cool under cold running water.
  Drain and dry the arugula and tear it by hand.
  Peel the peppers and cut into thin strips.
  Mix the cooled pasta with the peppers, arugula, and ricotta shavings. Season with olive oil, salt, and pepper and serve.

Note The best way to make cold pasta is to boil it in an abundance of salted water, drain when al dente, and then immediately rinse under cold running water or immerse in a bowl of ice water. Drain, then toss with a little oil so it does not become sticky.

Gnocchi with Speck, Peas, and Feta

Serves 4

3 tablespoons extra-virgin olive oil
1 shallot, minced
1⅓ cups (6 ounces) peas
1 thick slice speck (about 1 ounce) or smoked and cured ham, diced
salt and pepper
12½ ounces durum-wheat gnocchi or orechiette
2 ounces feta cheese, crumbled

Preparation time 10 minutes
Cooking time 20 minutes
Level easy
Wine young, medium-bodied rosé with marked floral bouquet,
such as Alto Adige Lagrein Rosé

Heat the oil and sauté the shallot with a little water. Add the peas and cook for 4 minutes over low heat. Add the speck and 1 ladleful of hot water. Cook for another 2 to 3 minutes.

Cook the pasta in a large pot of salted boiling water until al dente. Drain and add to the pan with the peas and speck. Let them absorb the liquid from the sauce, then sprinkle in the feta. Finish with a sprinkling of pepper and serve.

Note The feta can be replaced by 2 tablespoons fresh ricotta, mixed with a little of the liquid from the sauce, then added to the sauce with the pasta. This will make the sauce creamier.

Whole-Wheat Shells with Creamy Peppers

Serves 4

2 red bell peppers
3 tablespoons extra-virgin olive oil
1 shallot, minced
1 garlic clove
¾ cup plus 1 tablespoon heavy cream
salt and pepper
3 tablespoons grated Parmesan cheese
11½ ounces whole-wheat medium shells
1 wild fennel or dill sprig, minced

Preparation time 15 minutes
Cooking time 30 minutes
Level easy
Wine well-structured white with evolved bouquet, such as Campania Falanghina

Roast the peppers over an open flame until blackened. Close in a plastic bag and leave to steam for 10 minutes. Peel and seed the peppers, rinse and cut into strips.

Heat the olive oil and sauté the shallot with the whole garlic clove. Add the pepper strips (reserving a few for garnish) and the cream. Season with salt, add ½ cup water, and let cook for 20 minutes over low heat.

Remove the garlic clove, and puree the peppers and cream with an immersion blender or in a food processor. Add the Parmesan and season with salt and pepper.

Cook the pasta in a large pot of salted boiling water until al dente. Drain and toss with the pepper cream. Add the wild fennel and the reserved pepper strips. Stir well and serve hot.

Fusilli with Radicchio, Artichokes, and Speck

Serves 4

2 small artichokes
14 ounces dried egg fusilli
4 tablespoons extra-virgin olive oil
2 garlic cloves, unpeeled and halved
2½ ounces speck (or smoked and cured ham), cut into matchsticks
1 head radicchio, thinly sliced
salt and pepper
parsley, minced
3 tablespoons shaved aged ricotta

Preparation time 10 minutes
Cooking time 15 minutes
Level easy
Wine medium-structured red with developing bouquet of red fruits, such as Pinot Noir

Trim the artichokes, cutting off the tips and stems and removing the hard external leaves. Remove the choke and slice thinly (photo 1), then set aside.

Cook the pasta in a large pot of salted boiling water until al dente. Meanwhile heat the oil and sauté the garlic until golden. Add the speck (photo 2) and sauté, then add the artichokes (photo 3) and sauté over high heat.

Add the radicchio and season with salt and pepper. Add a little of the pasta cooking water and sprinkle with minced parsley.

Drain the pasta and add to the pan with the sauce. Sauté briefly, reducing the sauce, then serve topped with the ricotta shavings.

Rotelle with Fresh Tomato Sauce

Serves 4

10½ ounces rotelle (wheel-shaped pasta)
3 tablespoons extra-virgin olive oil
15 tomatoes, chopped
fresh aromatic herbs, as desired
10 basil leaves
salt and pepper
1 spring onion, thinly sliced

Preparation time 10 minutes
Cooking time 10 minutes
Level easy
Wine white with well-structured body and long persistence on the palate, such as Sicily Inzolia

Bring a large pot of water to a boil, salt, then add the pasta and cook until al dente. Drain and toss with 1 tablespoon olive oil, then let cool.

Place the tomatoes in a food processor with the remaining olive oil, the aromatic herbs, and the basil. Puree until smooth. Season with salt and pepper, then toss with the pasta.

Top the pasta with spring onion and serve.

Note The pasta can also be drained and tossed directly with the tomatoes for a hot dish that is still refreshing, thanks to the uncooked fresh tomatoes. This recipe works particularly well in the summer, with juicy tomatoes at the peak of ripeness.

Casarecce with Clams and Zucchini

Serves 4

1 pound clams
3 tablespoons extra-virgin olive oil
1 garlic clove, minced
½ dried red chili pepper, crumbled
1 zucchini, seeded and diced
10 cherry tomatoes, quartered
parsley, minced
salt
14 ounces casarecce (or campanelle)

Preparation time 20 minutes
Cooking time 15 minutes
Level medium
Wine medium-bodied white with bouquet of yellow fruits,
such as Friuli Tocai

Wash the clams well under cold running water, scrubbing them with a stiff brush. Let them soak in cold salted water for at least an hour.

Heat the olive oil in a frying pan and sauté the garlic with the chili pepper. Add the zucchini and brown for 1 minute, then add the clams. Cover and cook over high heat until the clams open, adding the tomatoes after a couple of minutes. Sprinkle with parsley.

Shell the clams and return them to the sauce.

Cook the pasta in a large pot of salted boiling water and cook until still very al dente. Drain and add directly to the clams. Sauté in the pan to reduce the sauce. Serve hot.

Cavatappi with Morels, Pecorino, and Nutmeg

Serves 4

4 fresh morel mushrooms (or dried and soaked until soft)
2 tablespoons butter
1 shallot, minced
vegetable broth
5½ ounces mild pecorino cheese, grated
7 tablespoons milk
nutmeg
salt and freshly ground pepper
10½ ounces spinach or whole-wheat cavatappi

Preparation time 15 minutes
Cooking time 20 minutes
Level medium
Wine fresh, young red with light body,
such as Veneto Bardolino Classico

Clean the morels well with a little paintbrush to remove all the dirt. Trim and discard the hard part of the stalk, and chop the rest of the stalk and the caps.

Melt the butter in a frying pan and sauté the shallot, then add the morels and cook for 5 minutes over low heat. Add a little broth or water.

Melt the pecorino with the milk in the top of a double boiler, without boiling. Grate in nutmeg to taste.

Cook the pasta in a large pot of salted boiling water until al dente. Drain, transfer to the pan with the mushrooms, and toss to coat. Sprinkle with a little freshly ground pepper, then divide between 4 serving dishes. Pour the hot cheese sauce over the pasta and serve.

Note Morels are one of the most highly prized wild mushrooms, excellent whether fresh or dried. Other mushrooms can be used for this recipe, though it's best not to select ones that have a strong flavor, as they will overpower the cheese and nutmeg.

Sardinian Gnocchi with Peas, Speck, and Saffron

Serves 4

4 tablespoons extra-virgin olive oil
1 small onion, diced
2⅓ cups (5 ounces) shelled peas
1 pinch ground saffron
3½ ounces speck, thickly sliced and diced
7 tablespoons whipping cream
salt and pepper
12½ ounces Sardinian gnocchi
2 tablespoons grated Parmesan

Preparation time 10 minutes
Cooking time 15 minutes
Level easy
Wine light and fresh young rosé, such as Tuscany Sangiovese

Heat the oil in a large frying pan and add the onion. Sauté without letting the onion color. Add the peas and cook for a few minutes. Pour over ½ cup of water, cover and cook for 15 minutes.

Dissolve the saffron in a little warm water. Add the speck to the peas, and then the cream. Simmer for 10 minutes. Finally, add the saffron and season to taste with salt and pepper.

Bring a large pot of salted water to a boil and add the pasta. Cook until al dente, drain and add to the sauce. Sauté the pasta in the sauce for a few minutes and sprinkle with grated Parmesan. Mix and serve immediately.

Note Add a little of the pasta cooking water to 2 tablespoons ricotta and mix until smooth. Add the ricotta cream to the pasta and the sauce before serving.

Long Pasta

From the classic spaghetti and linguine to tagliatelle and pappardelle, long pastas are true icons of Italian cuisine. And infinite variations are possible, thanks to a range of flavorful ragùs and other delicious sauces.

Spaghetti with Garlic, Oil, and Chili Pepper

Serves 4

3 garlic cloves
8 tablespoons extra-virgin olive oil
1 mild red chili pepper
salt
12½ ounces spaghetti alla chitarra or thick spaghetti

Preparation time 5 minutes
Cooking time 7 minutes
Level medium
Wine medium-bodied, well-structured white,
such as Sicily Bianco d'Alcamo

Peel the garlic cloves, remove the inner shoot, and puree the cloves in a food processor with 3 tablespoons olive oil. Let sit for 1 day in a cool place, then strain.
   Remove the seeds from the chili pepper, mince, and cook in a small saucepan with 3 tablespoons olive oil until it dissolves and becomes a paste.
   Cook the pasta in a large pot of salted boiling water until al dente. Drain and divide among 3 small bowls.
   Toss a third of the spaghetti with the garlic oil, a third with the chili paste, and a third with the remaining olive oil.
   Divide the spaghetti among 4 plates, forming small nests of each type of spaghetti, so that each plate has one of each flavor.

Note Here is the traditional recipe for this simple classic dish: While the spaghetti cooks, sauté 2 minced garlic cloves in some extra-virgin olive oil in a frying pan. When the garlic starts to turn color, add as many dried red chili flakes as desired and 2 tablespoons minced parsley, then after a few seconds, 1 ladleful of pasta cooking water. Drain the spaghetti when al dente and finish cooking in the frying pan with the sauce, thickening the sauce and infusing the pasta with more flavor.

Linguine with Walnuts and Arugula

Serves 4

½ cup shelled walnuts
1 tablespoon extra-virgin olive oil
salt
½ cup vegetable broth
11 ounces linguine
1 bunch arugula, shredded

Preparation time 15 minutes
Cooking time 15 minutes
Level easy
Wine well-structured white with a fully developed bouquet, such as Piedmont Riesling Renano

WALNUTS
Walnuts are a good luck charm. The Ancient Romans threw walnuts over newly married couples, a tradition that was still performed in Sicily at the beginning of the twentieth century. In Belgium, girls would mix whole walnuts with empty walnut shells; according to legend, those who picked a whole one would marry young.

Chop the walnuts coarsely with a mezzaluna or knife.
   In a small frying pan, toast the walnuts with the olive oil and a pinch of salt. Add the broth and reduce.
   Cook the linguine in a large pot of salted boiling until al dente. Drain and toss with the arugula, then add to the walnuts in the pan. Serve hot.

Note This simple recipe is both easy and fast. The sweet walnuts provide a delicious contrast to the bitter taste of the arugula. For more flavor, add shaved Pecorino Romano, or for a creamier version with a touch of acidity, 1 tablespoon of any soft spreadable cheese.

Pappardelle with Vegetable Ragù

Serves 4

2 small artichokes
juice of 1 lemon
4 tablespoons extra-virgin olive oil
1 large leek, diced
2 garlic cloves, smashed
1 small eggplant, peeled and diced
2 zucchini, diced
6 basil leaves, torn
10 black olives in oil, pitted
salt and pepper
10½ ounces dried egg pappardelle

Preparation time 25 minutes
Cooking time 30 minutes
Level easy
Wine light, young white with herbaceous undertones,
such as Friuli Malvasia Istriana

Clean the artichokes, removing the tough outer leaves and the choke from each. Dice and immerse in water and lemon juice.

Heat half of the olive oil in a frying pan and gently sauté the leek until soft but not browned. Add the artichokes and sauté over high heat for a few minutes. Add a little water and cook, covered, for 15 minutes.

In another frying pan, heat the remaining olive oil and the garlic. Sauté first the eggplant with a pinch of salt until tender, then remove from the pan and sauté the zucchini with a pinch of salt. Transfer the eggplant and zucchini to the artichokes and cook for 5 minutes. Add the basil, olives, and a pinch of pepper.

Cook the pasta in a large pot of salted boiling water until al dente. Drain, reserving a little of the cooking water. Toss the pappardelle with the sauce, adding a little of the reserved cooking water. Serve immediately.

Note This pasta sauce can be varied by adding different vegetables such as green beans, peas, broccoli, or snow peas. The vegetables should be chopped into matchstick-sized pieces and then sautéed until tender. Baby spinach and zucchini blossoms may be added when the vegetables are nearly cooked.

Vermicelli with Tuna and Tomato Sauce

Serves 4

4 ripe tomatoes (about 14 ounces)
3 tablespoons extra-virgin olive oil
½ onion, minced
1 bunch of parsley, minced
salt and pepper
7 ounces tuna in oil, drained and crumbled
14 ounces vermicelli

Preparation time 5 minutes
Cooking time 20 minutes
Level easy
Wine full-bodied, structured white with a well-developed bouquet, such as Sicily Chardonnay Barrique

Blanch the tomatoes briefly in boiling water. Drain, peel, and deseed them, then thinly slice.
  Heat the extra-virgin olive oil in a wide frying pan and sauté the onion and parsley. Add the sliced tomatoes and adjust salt and pepper. Cook for about 15 minutes, stirring every so often. Stir in the tuna.
  Bring a large pot of salted water to the boil and cook the vermicelli until al dente. Drain and toss in the frying pan with the sauce. Stir well, then serve immediately.

Note The vermicelli can be replaced with 12½ ounces ridged pennette.

Black Tagliolini with Baby Squid and Artichokes

Serves 4

3 ½ ounces baby squid, cleaned
3 tablespoons extra-virgin olive oil
1 shallot, minced
3 artichoke hearts, thinly sliced
1 zucchini, julienned
7 tablespoons fish broth
10 cherry tomatoes, sliced
salt and pepper
12 ½ ounces dried black tagliolini or linguine

Preparation time 20 minutes
Cooking time 25 minutes
Level easy
Wine full-bodied, structured white with a well-developed,
such as bouquet Campania Greco di Tufo

Wash the baby squid well.
  Heat the olive oil in a large frying pan and add the shallot. Cook over low heat until soft. Add the artichokes and sauté for 5 minutes. Raise the heat and add the zucchini and the baby squid. Stir the mixture with a wooden spoon and add the fish broth and tomatoes. Season to taste with salt and pepper.
  Cook the pasta in a large pot of salted boiling water until al dente, then drain. Transfer to the pan with the sauce and sauté quickly, shaking the pan to thoroughly coat. Remove from the heat and serve immediately.

Variation Add julienned carrot, thinly sliced beetroot, and a few wild arugula leaves to this pasta for more color.

Farro Spaghetti with Cauliflower and Olives

Serves 4

1 small cauliflower, cut into florets
salt
12 ounces farro spaghetti
3 tablespoons extra-virgin olive oil
1 shallot, minced
1 tablespoon capers
10 green olives, pitted
chives, chopped
basil, shredded
toasted sunflower seeds

FARRO PASTA

Pasta made from farro (emmer wheat) should always be drained while it is still very al dente. This type of pasta doesn't maintain its consistency after cooking because it is dried at a very low temperature; also, the gluten in farro has a different structure than in durum wheat.

Preparation time 15 minutes
Cooking time 20 minutes
Level easy
Wine young, medium-bodied and pleasantly acidic rosé, such as Alto Adige Lagrein Rosato

Blanch the cauliflower florets for a few minutes in boiling salted water.

Cook the farro spaghetti in a large pot of salted boiling water for 10 minutes. Meanwhile heat 2 tablespoons olive oil in a frying pan and sauté the shallot with the capers and olives. Add the cauliflower.

Drain the spaghetti and add to the sauce. Cook for a few minutes, then drizzle with olive oil and sprinkle with chives and basil. Serve topped with toasted sunflower seeds.

Note Farro pasta lends itself to many vegetable sauces. Try the following variation: gently sauté 1 thinly sliced leek in extra-virgin olive oil in a heavy-bottomed pan. Add a diced turnip and some diced pancetta. Let cook until the fat begins to render and then add a few tablespoons of hot water or vegetable broth. Add a generous handful of broccoli rabe. Cook for 7 to 8 minutes. Boil the pasta in salted water until al dente and add it to the vegetables. Sauté briefly and serve.

Fettuccine with Ricotta-Lime Sauce and Turbot

Serves 4

Turbot
4 turbot fillets (about 4½ ounces each)
¼ cup hazelnuts
parsley sprigs
2 tablespoons light extra-virgin olive oil
1 garlic clove, smashed

Fettuccine
salt and pepper
6½ ounces dried egg fettuccine
3 ounces ricotta salata cheese, crumbled
grated zest of 1 lime
2 tablespoons butter

Preparation time 20 minutes
Cooking time 25 minutes
Level medium
Wine medium-bodied white with hints of citrus,
such as Sicily Catarratto

Cut the turbot fillets in half diagonally, then trim them to form 8 diamond shapes.
Toast the hazelnuts in a nonstick frying pan then finely chop.
Dip 4 of the turbot fillet pieces in the chopped hazelnuts and set aside.
Place remaining 4 pieces of turbot in a steaming basket with some parsley sprigs. Steam over hot water until cooked through.
Heat a nonstick frying pan with the olive oil and garlic. Sauté the hazelnut-coated turbot until browned.
Cook the fettuccine in a large pot of salted boiling water until al dente. Drain and transfer to a bowl. Toss with the ricotta salata, lime zest, and butter.
Compose each serving portion, making towers with 1 hazelnut-crusted turbot piece, some fettuccine, and 1 steamed turbot piece. Sprinkle with pepper and serve.

Pasta Nests with Squash Blossoms and Baby Squid

Serves 4

7 ounces baby squid
10 squash blossoms
4 tablespoons extra-virgin olive oil
1 shallot, minced
1 pinch dried red chili pepper flakes
½ cup fish broth
salt and freshly ground pepper
1 slice Tuscan-style bread, diced
12½ ounces spaghetti alla chitarra or thick spaghetti

Preparation time 20 minutes
Cooking time 15 minutes
Level easy
Wine well-structured, medium-bodied, young white,
such as Campania Fiano di Avellino

Wash the baby squid in an abundance of cold water, removing the central bone. Drain and set aside.

Wipe the squash blossoms with a damp paper towel, remove the inner yellow pistil, and cut off the stalk.

Heat the olive oil in a frying pan and sauté the shallot with a pinch of chili pepper flakes until soft. Add the squash blossom and cook for 3 minutes, adding a little fish broth. Add the baby squid and season with salt and pepper. Continue cooking until squid are cooked through.

Meanwhile toast the bread under the broiler or in a hot oven.

Cook the spaghetti in a large pot of salted boiling water. Drain when still very al dente. Transfer to the pan with the sauce and continue cooking until spaghetti is done. Add the toasted bread.

Form nests of the pasta using a large fork and a wide ladle. Serve with a generous sprinkling of freshly ground pepper.

Note The *chitarra* is a tool from Abruzzo used to make spaghetti alla chitarra. It consists of a wooden frame strung with metal wire, like a guitar. Sheets of fresh pasta are placed on top of the strings and then rolled with a large rolling pin, pushing them through and forming spaghetti with a square cross-section.

Corn Tagliatelle with Porcini, Swordfish, and Thyme

Serves 4

2 small porcini mushrooms
11 ounces corn tagliatelle or fettuccine
3 tablespoons extra-virgin olive oil
½ red chili pepper
2 garlic cloves
1 sprig thyme, minced
7 ounces swordfish fillets, skinned and diced
salt and pepper

Preparation time 20 minutes
Cooking time 20 minutes
Level easy
Wine young, light-bodied red with grassy undertones,
such as Alto Adige Pinot Noir

Carefully clean the porcini with a damp paper towel, then cut into thin slices.
  Cook the pasta in a large pot of salted boiling water until al dente. At the same time, heat the olive oil in a frying pan with the chili pepper and garlic, then add the porcini and sauté. Sprinkle with thyme, then add the swordfish. Cook for another 5 minutes, adding a little pasta cooking water, and season with salt and pepper. Drain the pasta and transfer to the pan with the sauce. Stir, then serve immediately.

Note Corn meal is a gluten-free source of complex carbohydrates, essential amino acids, and vitamin E. It is thought to have calming and detoxifying effects on the body.

Tagliolini with Scallops, Lentils, and Lime

Serves 4

¾ cup (5 ounces) Castelluccio or other small brown lentils
2 garlic cloves, 1 unpeeled, whole and 1 peeled, minced
12 scallops
8 tablespoons extra-virgin olive oil
½ red chili pepper, minced
2 tablespoons brandy
parsley, minced
1 tomato, chopped
salt and pepper
13½ ounces dried egg tagliolini (or linguine)
grated zest of 1 lime

Preparation time 25 minutes
Cooking time 25 minutes
Difficulty easy
Wine medium-bodied white with a full and fragrant bouquet, such as Tuscany Chardonnay

Wash the lentils under running water. Boil them with a little salt and 1 unpeeled garlic clove until al dente, then drain.

While the lentils are cooking, wash the scallops and cut into small pieces, leaving the red roe (coral) intact. Heat the olive oil in a frying pan and sauté the minced garlic and chili pepper.

When the lentils are done, start to bring a large pot of water to a boil in preparation for the pasta. Add the lentils to the garlic and chili pepper and stir well, then add the scallops. Add the brandy, let evaporate, then sprinkle with parsley. Add the tomato, sauté for a few moments, then adjust salt and pepper to taste.

Salt the boiling water, add the pasta, and cook until still quite al dente. Drain, then transfer to the pan with the lentils and scallops, together with the lime zest. Cook briefly, then serve.

Spaghetti with Squash Blossoms and Squid

Serves 4

1 pound medium-small squid, cleaned
8 squash blossoms
3 tablespoons extra-virgin olive oil
1 shallot, minced
4 baby zucchini, julienned
1 large carrot, peeled and julienned
vegetable broth
parsley, minced
salt and pepper
13 ½ ounces spaghetti alla chitarra or thick spaghetti

Preparation time 25 minutes
Cooking time 25 minutes
Difficulty easy
Wine medium-bodied white with a bouquet of yellow fruits, such as Marches Verdicchio dei Castelli di Jesi

Wash the squid well, and cut it into rings.
   Wipe the squash blossoms with a damp paper towel, then remove the inner pistil and the stalk. Coarsely chop the blossoms.
   Bring a large pot of water to a boil, then salt.
   Meanwhile heat the olive oil and gently sauté the shallot until soft. Add the zucchini and carrot. Sauté briefly, then add the squash blossoms. Add a little vegetable broth, then the squid. Sprinkle with parsley and season with salt and pepper.
   Cook the spaghetti until al dente. Drain, transfer to the pan with the sauce, and toss to coat.

Variation The spaghetti can also be tossed with a sauce made from puntarelle (a type of chicory), blanched and sautéed in olive oil with chili peppers, cherry tomatoes, and squid rings.

Vermicelli with Potatoes and Parsley

Serves 6

2 medium potatoes
salt
1 pound vermicelli
3 tablespoons extra-virgin olive oil
1 bunch of parsley, minced
freshly ground black pepper

Preparation time 5 minutes
Cooking time 15 minutes
Level easy
Wine young and light-bodied white with an herbaceous bouquet, such as Friuli Ribolla Gialla

Peel the potatoes, dice them, and boil in abundant salted water. When the potatoes are al dente, add the vermicelli to the water. Cook for another 6 to 7 minutes, then drain and transfer to a serving dish. Drizzle with oil and toss with freshly ground black pepper and parsley.

Variation Enrich the taste of this dish by adding a bunch of arugula to the potatoes together with the vermicelli. Garnish the finished dish with a pinch of chili pepper flakes and shavings of ricotta salata.

Spaghetti with Clams and Cuttlefish

Serves 4

2¼ pounds small clams
4 tablespoons extra-virgin olive oil
7 ounces cuttlefish, cleaned and cut into strips
1 leek, sliced into rings
½ cup white wine
1 bunch parsley, stemmed and minced
1 garlic clove
salt and pepper
14 ounces spaghetti

Preparation time 30 minutes
Cooking time 30 minutes
Level medium
Wine young, medium-bodied white with sustained acidity, such as Liguria Vermentino

Wash the clams well under cold running water, scrubbing them with a stiff brush. Let them soak in cold salted water for at least an hour.

Heat 3 tablespoons olive oil and sauté the cuttlefish and leek (photo 1). Let brown for 5 minutes. Add the white wine and continue cooking for 10 minutes.

Heat 1 tablespoon oil in a frying pan with 1 tablespoon minced parsley and the garlic clove, and add the clams. Cover and cook until opened. Shell half the clams (photo 2) and add to the cuttlefish.

Cook the spaghetti in a large pot of salted boiling water until al dente. Drain, transfer to the pan with the cuttlefish, and sauté over high heat for a few minutes (photo 3).

Top the spaghetti with the clams in shells sprinkled with a little pepper and the remaining parsley, and serve.

Spaghetti Nests with Asparagus and Chinese Cabbage

Serves 4

2 tablespoons extra-virgin olive oil
15 asparagus spears (about 9 ounces), sliced on the diagonal
salt and freshly ground pepper
5½ ounces strong Gorgonzola cheese, chopped
2 tablespoons black sesame seeds
10½ ounces spaghetti alla chitarra or thick spaghetti
2½ cups (7 ounces) shredded Chinese cabbage
⅓ cup butter

Preparation time 15 minutes
Cooking time 20 minutes
Difficulty easy
Wine young, medium-bodied white with sustained acidity, such as Liguria Vermentino

Heat the olive oil in a frying pan and sauté the asparagus slices with a pinch of salt until crisp-tender. Add the Gorgonzola and a little water. Let the cheese melt over low heat then set aside.

Toast the sesame seeds in a nonstick frying pan or in the oven for a few minutes.

Cook the spaghetti in a large pot of salted boiling water until al dente. Halfway through the cooking time, add the Chinese cabbage. Drain the spaghetti and cabbage and transfer to the pan with the asparagus, together with a little of the cooking water. Add the butter and return to the heat. Sauté, stirring well, until all the ingredients are combined.

Sprinkle with freshly ground pepper and sesame seeds, then serve immediately.

Corn Tagliatelle with Shrimp and Zucchini

Serves 4

10½ ounces shrimp
2 small baby zucchini with flowers attached
3 tablespoons extra-virgin olive oil
1 garlic clove, halved and inner shoot removed
½ red chili pepper, seeded
7 to 8 cherry tomatoes, quartered and seeded
salt and pepper
9 ounces corn tagliatelle or fettuccine
parsley, minced

Preparation time 20 minutes
Cooking time 20 minutes
Level easy
Wine young, medium-bodied white with a bouquet of yellow fruits, such as Campania Greco di Tufo

Shell and devein the shrimp (photo 1), and chop.

Detach the flowers from the zucchini, wipe with a damp paper towel, remove the inner pistil, and set aside the flowers.

Cut the zucchini lengthwise into quarters, then remove and discard the inner white part. Julienne the rest (photo 2).

Heat the olive oil and sauté the garlic and chili pepper, then add the zucchini and tomatoes. Remove the garlic and sauté over high heat. Move the vegetables to one side of the pan and add the shrimp to the other. Continue to cook over high heat. Add the flowers and season with salt and pepper.

Cook the pasta in a large pot of salted boiling water until al dente. Drain and add to the pan with the vegetables and shrimp, and mix well.

Sprinkle with parsley and serve.

Farro Tagliatelle with Spring Onions and Asparagus

Serves 4

3 tablespoons extra-virgin olive oil
4 spring onions, sliced
salt and freshly ground pepper
3½ ounces robiola cheese or fresh goat cheese
2 tablespoons grated Parmesan
8 asparagus spears, sliced on the diagonal
10½ ounces farro tagliatelle or fettuccine
4 sprigs curly parsley

Preparation time 40 minutes
Cooking tim 30 minutes
Level easy
Wine Light-bodied, fresh and fruity, such as red Friuli Merlot

Heat 1 tablespoon olive oil in a frying pan and sauté the spring onions with a pinch of salt. Pour in a glass of water and let cook for about 20 minutes.

Remove the spring onions from the heat and puree in a food processor or blender. Add the robiola and Parmesan and puree for a few more seconds, then season with salt and pepper to taste.

Heat 2 tablespoons olive oil in a frying pan and sauté the asparagus with a little salt for a few minutes over high heat. Remove from the heat and set aside.

Cook the pasta in a large pot of salted boiling water until al dente. Drain and add to the pan with the asparagus, together with a little of the cooking water. Add the spring onion puree, stir carefully, then serve, sprinkled with freshly ground pepper and garnished with a parsley sprig.

Spaghettoni with Tomatoes, Anchovies, and Capers

Serves 4

12 fresh anchovies
2 firm vine-ripened tomatoes
3 tablespoons extra-virgin olive oil
2 garlic cloves, smashed
1 spring onion, sliced
8 salted capers, rinsed
pinch fresh oregano leaves
1 tablespoon parsley, minced
salt and pepper
12½ ounces rough-textured spaghettoni, or thick spaghetti, or bucatini rigati (thick spaghetti)

CAPERS
Caper bushes grow along the sea coast in Mediterranean countries, and capers are the pickled or salted flower buds. The fruits, known as caperberries (see photo above), look like gherkins and are excellent preserved in vinegar and served as a snack with drinks.

Preparation time 15 minutes
Cooking time 10 minutes
Level easy
Wine full-bodied, structured white with an evolved bouquet, such as Sicily Chardonnay Barrique

Wash the anchovies under cold running water. Open them like a book, removing the head and backbone from each, and rinse.

Cut an X on the bottom of the tomatoes and blanch them in boiling water for 1 minute. Drain and immerse in ice water. Drain, peel, remove the seeds, and dice.

Heat the olive oil in a frying pan and gently sauté the garlic with the spring onion and capers. Add the anchovies, then the tomatoes, and turn up the heat. Add the oregano and parsley and season with salt and pepper to taste.

Cook the pasta in a large pot of salted boiling water until very al dente. Drain, reserving 2 cups cooking water. Transfer the pasta to the pan with the sauce and sauté, adding cooking water little by little.

Cook over high heat until the pasta finishes cooking, then serve.

Note This recipe requires a very thick pasta. With such a strong sauce, a thinner pasta risks being completely overwhelmed, losing its own flavor and disrupting the balance of the dish.

Spaghetti alla Chitarra with Swordfish Ragù

Serves 4

7 tablespoons extra-virgin olive oil
9 ounces swordfish, diced
1 garlic clove
1⅓ cups cherry tomatoes, halved
1 eggplant, diced
salt and pepper
12½ ounces spaghetti alla chitarra (or thick spaghetti)
1 mint sprig, minced
fresh basil, minced
parsley, minced
1 red chili pepper, minced

Preparation time 20 minutes
Cooking time 25 minutes
Level easy
Wine full-bodied white with fragrant notes of mature fruit, such as Sicily Inzolia

Heat 2 tablespoons of olive oil in a frying pan. Add the swordfish, season with salt, and sauté for 2 minutes.

In another frying pan heat 3 tablespoons of olive oil and add the garlic clove. When the garlic begins to brown, remove it and add the cooked swordfish, cherry tomatoes, and eggplant. Season the sauce with salt and pepper and continue cooking until the eggplant is tender.

Meanwhile, bring a large pot of salted water to a boil. Add the spaghetti alla chitarra and cook until al dente. Drain and transfer to the pan with the sauce.

Sauté the pasta and the sauce briefly and add the minced herbs, chili pepper, and 2 tablespoons of oil. Toss to coat and serve.

Note The cherry tomatoes may be substituted with canned crushed tomatoes.

Spaghetti with Shrimp and Green Beans

Serves 4

1½ cups (6½ ounces) green beans
12 large shrimp
2 tablespoons extra-virgin olive oil
1 garlic clove, minced
½ red chili pepper, minced
1 tablespoon parsley, minced
salt
½ cup white wine
8 large squash blossoms, sliced
1 tomato, seeded and chopped
14 ounces spaghetti alla chitarra or thick spaghetti

Preparation time 15 minutes
Cooking time 25 minutes
Difficulty easy
Wine méthode champenoise with full body and well-rounded structure, such as Champagne Brut

Trim the green beans and blanch in boiling salted water for 4 minutes.

Halve the shrimp lengthwise, removing the legs but leaving the shell. Heat the oil in a frying pan and sauté the garlic, chili pepper, and parsley. Add the shrimp and sauté, season with salt, then add the wine. As soon as the wine has evaporated, add the green beans and squash blossoms. Add a little water and continue cooking for a few minutes, covered, to blend all the flavors, then stir in the tomato.

Cook the pasta in a large pot of salted boiling water until al dente. Drain and toss with the sauce, adding a little of the cooking water or shrimp broth.

Linguine with Cherry Tomatoes, Raisins, and Pine Nuts

Serves 4

¼ cup (1 ounce) raisins
⅓ cup (1½ ounce) pine nuts
extra-virgin olive oil
5 tablespoons breadcrumbs
1 garlic clove
2 cups (10½ ounces) cherry tomatoes, halved
14 ounces linguine
mint, basil, and marjoram, chopped
salt and pepper

Preparation time 10 minutes
Cooking time 5 minutes
Level easy
Wine young, medium-bodied, pleasantly acidic white, such as Liguria Pigato

Soak the raisins in warm water for 15 minutes. Meanwhile, toast the pine nuts in a nonstick frying pan with a little olive oil for 1 minute. Toast the breadcrumbs in a nonstick frying pan or under a broiler and set aside.

Heat a few tablespoons of olive oil in a large frying pan and add the whole garlic clove. Add the cherry tomatoes, pine nuts, and drained raisins and season to taste with salt and pepper. Cook over high heat for 5 minutes. Remove from the heat and discard the garlic clove.

Bring a large pot of salted water to a boil and add the linguine. Cook until al dente, drain and add to the pan with the sauce. Sauté the pasta briefly in the sauce and sprinkle over the toasted breadcrumbs and chopped herbs.

Serve the pasta, if desired, with shaved ricotta salata.

Linguine with Octopus and Artichokes

Serves 4

1 1/3 pound octopus
5 tablespoons extra-virgin olive oil
1 garlic clove, smashed
3 artichokes
1 bunch parsley, stemmed and minced
1/2 cup vegetable broth
salt and pepper
12 1/2 ounces linguine

Preparation time 30 minutes
Cooking time 40 minutes
Level easy
Wine well-structured white with pronounced fruity aromas, such as Campania Fiano di Avellino

Slice the octopus into small rounds.
    Heat 2 1/2 tablespoons olive oil in a large nonstick frying pan with the garlic clove. Add the octopus and sauté for 15 minutes over medium heat.
    Meanwhile, trim the artichokes, removing and discarding the tough outer leaves and inner choke from each, then thinly slice.
    Add the artichokes and minced parsley to the pan with the octopus, then add the vegetable broth. Season with salt. Continue cooking for 10 to 12 minutes.
    Cook the pasta in a large pot of salted boiling water until al dente, then drain. Transfer to the pan with the sauce and sauté for 1 minute. Season with freshly ground pepper and drizzle with olive oil. Serve immediately.

Note It is important that the pasta finish cooking in the octopus sauce. The linguine will absorb the flavors of the sauce, and as it cooks, the starch from the pasta will make the sauce thick and creamy.

Linguine with Shellfish

Serves 4

4½ ounces mussels
4½ ounces cockles
4½ ounces Manila clams
4 ounces littleneck clams
  or other small clams
3 tablespoons extra-virgin olive oil
1 garlic clove, minced
1 red chili pepper, minced
6 to 7 baby plum tomatoes, quartered
parsley, minced
salt
11 ounces linguine

Preparation time 15 minutes
Cooking time 15 minutes
Level easy
Wine full-bodied, structured white with elegant flavors,
such as Tuscany Chardonnay

Wash all of the different shellfish separately in cold water. Scrub and debeard the mussels. Let all of the clams soak separately in salted cold water for 30 minutes.

Meanwhile, heat the olive oil in a frying pan and add the garlic and chili pepper. Add the cockles, and then the Manila clams. Let cook for 3 minutes, then add the littleneck clams and mussels. Cover and cook for 3 more minutes. Add the tomatoes and sprinkle with some minced parsley. Remove the shellfish from the pan and place on a plate with a little of the cooking liquid. Cover to keep warm.

Cook the linguine in a large pot of salted boiling water for 5 minutes. Drain and add to the pan with the tomatoes. Sauté the pasta in the sauce until the pasta is al dente and the sauce creamy. Add the shellfish and mix well. Serve immediately.

Vermicelli with Clams

Serves 4

3 pounds littleneck clams or other small clams
½ cup extra-virgin olive oil
salt and freshly ground pepper
2 small potatoes, peeled and diced
10½ ounces vermicelli
2 garlic cloves, smashed
1 bunch parsley, stemmed and minced

Preparation time 25 minutes
Cooking time 15 minutes
Level medium
Wine young, light-bodied white with a grassy bouquet, such as Veneto Lugana

Wash the clams well under cold running water, scrubbing them with a stiff brush. Let them soak in cold salted water for at least an hour.

Heat 2 tablespoons olive oil in a frying pan and add the drained clams. Cover and cook over medium heat until all of the clams have opened. Remove from heat and shell the clams, discarding the shells and reserving the meat. Strain the liquid left in the pan and set aside.

Bring a large pot of water to a boil, add salt and then the potatoes. When the water returns to a boil, add the vermicelli. Heat the remaining olive oil in a large frying pan with the garlic cloves. Add the shelled clams, parsley, and reserved clam broth. Cook for 2 minutes, then remove the garlic cloves.

Drain the pasta when it is very al dente, reserving a few tablespoons of the cooking water. Add the pasta and the water to the clam sauce and cook over low heat for 2 minutes. Season with a good amount of freshly ground pepper and serve immediately.

Spaghettini with Broccoli Cream and Tuna

Serves 4

1 head broccoli, cut into florets
¼ cup extra-virgin olive oil
1 garlic clove
1 anchovy fillet in oil, drained
2 tablespoons grated Parmesan cheese
salt and pepper
12½ ounces fresh tuna fillet, diced
10½ ounces spaghettini (thin spaghetti)

Preparation time 10 minutes
Cooking time 15 minutes
Level easy
Wine well-structured, full-bodied white with a persistent bouquet, such as Sicily Catarratto

Blanch the broccoli in boiling salted water for 7 to 8 minutes. Drain the florets when they are still slightly crunchy and set a few aside.

Heat 2 tablespoons olive oil in a large frying pan. Add the garlic clove and anchovy. Add the broccoli florets and sauté until tender. Puree with an immersion blender and then strain the mixture. Add the Parmesan and season to taste with salt and pepper.

Heat the remaining olive oil in another frying pan and sauté the tuna very briefly. Season with a pinch of salt and add the reserved broccoli florets. Remove from heat.

Cook the spaghettini in a large pot of salted boiling water until al dente. Drain, reserving a few tablespoons of the cooking water. Add the pasta to the pan with the tuna and broccoli florets, and pour in the broccoli puree and cooking water. Mix well and serve immediately.

Note Tuna, swordfish, and sturgeon are best cooked rare. This maintains the delicate consistency and succulence of the meat. However, consuming raw or undercooked seafood may increase your risk of food-borne illness. To reduce this risk, you should ensure that your fish is as fresh as can be. It should smell only of the sea, not "fishy."

Baked Ziti with Tomatoes and Provolone

Serves 4

3 tablespoons extra-virgin olive oil
2 garlic cloves, smashed
10½ ounces canned peeled plum tomatoes
salt and pepper
14 ounces ziti
7 ounces fresh provolone cheese, diced (photo 2)
1 cup (3½ ounces) grated aged Pecorino Romano

Preparation time 15 minutes
Cooking time 20 minutes
Level easy
Wine well-structured, medium-bodied, young rosé, such as Veneto Bardolino Chiaretto

Preheat the oven to 425°F.
　Heat the olive oil in a saucepan and sauté the garlic until golden. Add the tomatoes and crush with the back of a wooden spoon. Cook over medium heat for 6 to 7 minutes and season with salt and pepper.
　Cook the ziti in a large pot of salted boiling water until al dente. Drain and toss with the tomatoes (photo 1). Stir in the provolone (photo 3) and half of the Pecorino. Place the pasta in a baking dish and sprinkle with the remaining Pecorino. Bake for 5 minutes and serve.

Variation For a lighter flavor, use buffalo mozzarella in place of the Pecorino cheese. Sprinkle the chopped cheese over the pasta as it comes out of the oven. The melted cheese will make the dish moist and creamy.

Tagliatelline with Zucchini and Shrimp

Serves 4

4 vine-ripened tomatoes
4 baby zucchini with flowers attached
5 tablespoons extra-virgin olive oil
1 shallot, minced
1 garlic clove, smashed
salt and pepper
10½ ounces large shrimp, shelled and diced
12½ ounces tagliatelline (thin tagliatelle) or thin fettuccine
10 basil leaves, julienned

Preparation time 20 minutes
Cooking time 15 minutes
Level easy
Wine light-bodied, fresh and fragrant white,
such as Alto Adige Pinot Grigio

Blanch the tomatoes, peel, seed, and dice.
   Remove and julienne the flowers from the zucchini, reserving a few whole flowers for garnish. Slice the zucchini.
   Heat the olive oil and sauté the shallot and garlic until soft. Add the zucchini, season with salt, and sauté over high heat for 2 to 3 minutes. Add the tomatoes and let cook for 5 minutes. Stir in the shrimp, remove from the heat, and keep warm.
   Cook the pasta in a large pot of salted boiling water until al dente. Drain the pasta, reserving a little cooking water, then add both to the pan with the sauce. Add the basil and season with pepper to taste. Drizzle with a little olive oil, sauté for a couple of minutes over high heat, then serve, garnished with the reserved flowers.

Variation If you buy whole, large shrimp, the shells and heads can be used to add more flavor to the sauce. Sauté 1 minced shallot and 1 garlic clove in a little extra-virgin olive oil, add the shrimp shells and heads, and brown briefly. Add a little white wine, 1 chopped tomato, and 1 teaspoon tomato paste. Add a little water and cook for 20 minutes over medium heat. Pass through a food mill, pressing down on the shells and heads to extract as much flavor and liquid as possible. If there is too much liquid, cook it down. Add this reduced broth to the pasta sauce to give it a more intense flavor.

Bucatini Nests with Spicy Calamari

Serves 4

9 ounces small calamari, cleaned and sliced into rings
6 tablespoons extra-virgin olive oil
2 garlic cloves, minced
2 red chili peppers, minced
1 bunch parsley, stemmed and minced
¾ cup red wine
½ cup (4½ ounces) canned crushed tomatoes
1 rosemary sprig
salt and pepper
13½ ounces bucatini or spaghetti
1 small zucchini, seeded and julienned

Preparation time 20 minutes
Cooking time 25 minutes
Level easy
Wine medium-bodied white with a fragrant bouquet of yellow fruits, such as Umbria Orvieto Classico

Heat the olive oil in a large frying pan and add the minced garlic, chili peppers, and parsley. Sauté the mixture over low heat for a few minutes and then add the sliced calamari. When the calamari are hot, pour in the red wine. Add the crushed tomatoes and cook over low heat for 7 minutes. Add the rosemary sprig and season to taste with salt and pepper. Cover the pan and continue cooking for another 8 minutes.

Cook the pasta in a large pot of salted boiling water until al dente. Halfway through the cooking time, add the zucchini. Drain the pasta and zucchini.

Using a large fork, make little nests of pasta and zucchini on individual serving plates. Top with the calamari sauce and serve immediately.

Special Recipes

Italy's top chefs reveal
their pasta secrets and share
some of the recipes
that made them famous.

Paccheri with Cuttlefish, Squid, and Sausage
from Moreno Cedroni

Serves 4

7 tablespoons extra-virgin olive oil
2 teaspoons minced garlic
5 ounces pork sausage, casing removed
7 ounce cuttlefish, cleaned and diced
3½ ounces squid, cleaned and diced
3½ ounces wild herbs and greens (young tender nettles or arugula), chopped
1 cup vegetable broth
salt
10½ ounces paccheri (or rigatoni)

Preparation time 10 minutes
Cooking time 15 minutes
Level medium
Wine medium-bodied white with fresh, fruity notes, such as Verdicchio dei Castelli di Jesi

Heat the oil in a frying pan and sauté the garlic. Crumble in the sausage meat. Brown lightly, then add the cuttlefish and squid. When the cuttlefish pieces have turned white, add the herbs and greens and the broth, and season with salt.

Cook the pasta in a large pot of salted boiling water until al dente. Drain and toss with the sauce, and continue cooking until the sauce is creamy.

Note Paccheri are a shape of pasta characteristic of the southern Italian region of Campania. In the past, they were known as "the pasta of the poor," because it took just a few to fill a plate. Traditionally they were sauced with San Marzano plum tomatoes, but these days they are often paired with fish or seafood sauces. The distinctive rough surface of the pasta helps hold the sauce and all its flavor. If you are unable to find paccheri or giant paccheri for this recipe, you may substitute rigatoni.

Bucatini all'Amatriciana with Balsamic Vinegar

from Angelo Troiani

Serves 4

3 to 4 tomatoes (about 14 ounces)
6 tablespoons extra-virgin olive oil
5 tablespoons minced onion
1 garlic clove
dried red chili pepper flakes
4½ ounces guanciale or pancetta, cut into matchsticks
1 tablespoon balsamic vinegar
salt
14 ounces bucatini or spaghetti
6 tablespoons grated Pecorino Romano cheese

Preparation time 10 minutes
Cooking time 20 minutes
Level easy
Wine structured red with an evolving, elegant and refined bouquet, such as Alto Adige Cabernet Sauvignon

Blanch the tomatoes, drain, immerse in cold water, then peel.
   Heat the olive oil in a frying pan and sauté the onion, garlic, and chili flakes until soft, then add the meat and brown.
   Add the balsamic vinegar and tomatoes. Season with salt and let simmer for 6 to 7 minutes.
   Cook the pasta in a large pot of salted boiling water until al dente. Drain and transfer to the pan with the sauce. Stir well until coated, then serve topped with grated Pecorino Romano.

Spaghetti with Soft-Shell Crabs
from Grazia Soncini

Serves 4

14 ounces soft-shell crabs
5 tablespoons extra-virgin olive oil
1 shallot, minced
2 tablespoons brandy
salt and freshly ground white pepper
3 tablespoons butter
1 pound turnip tops or broccoli rabe
1 garlic clove, unpeeled
dried red chili pepper flakes
10½ ounces spaghetti

Preparation time 30 minutes
Cooking time 30 minutes
Level easy
Wine Malvasia Istriana

Cut the crabs in half, reserving any liquid that comes out.
   Heat 2 tablespoons olive oil in a frying pan and gently sauté the shallot for a few minutes, then raise the heat and add the crabs. Cook them until they start to turn pink, then add the brandy. Cook off the alcohol, then remove from the heat. Sprinkle with a little freshly ground white pepper, then add the butter (without stirring) and cover.
   Blanch the turnip tops in boiling salted water, then drain.
   Heat the remaining olive oil in another frying pan and sauté the garlic and chili flakes until the garlic is browned. Remove the garlic, add the turnip tops, and sauté quickly.
   Cook the spaghetti in a large pot of salted boiling water until al dente. Drain and add to the pan with the crabs together with the turnip tops. Stir well and serve.

Note In Italian this type of crab is known as moleca (the plural form is moleche), which comes from the Venetian dialect and is used to refer to the male crab when it has shed its hard shell and can be eaten whole.

Mezze Maniche with Sea Urchin and Peas
from Lucio Pompili

Serves 4

1½ cups (7 ounces) sweet spring peas
6 tablespoons extra-virgin olive oil
vegetable broth
salt and black pepper
aged guanciale (or pancetta), cut into thin strips
1 onion, minced
1 garlic clove, minced
1 bunch fresh herbs, minced
½ cup (3½ ounces) fresh tomato puree
12½ ounces mezze maniche (or rigatoni)
½ cup sea urchin roe, also known as uni

Preparation time 15 minutes
Cooking time 25 minutes
Level medium
Wine Verdicchio dei Castelli di Jesi

Steam the peas or boil them in salted water until tender. Immediately immerse in ice water to maintain the color. Reserve some for garnish, then puree the rest with 5 tablespoons olive oil, using either an immersion blender or a food processor. If necessary, add a little vegetable broth to thin. Season with salt and pepper to taste.

Brown the meat in a nonstick frying pan until crispy. Remove from the pan and add the onion, garlic, and herbs. Add the tomato puree.

Cook the pasta in a large pot of salted boiling water until al dente. Drain and add to the pan with the tomatoes together with a little of the pea puree. Mix well. Place a little pea puree in the center of each individual plate. Using a round cookie cutter to help shape the portion, place some pasta on top. Garnish with sea urchin roe, a few pieces of crispy guanciale, and some of the reserved peas. Drizzle with a little olive oil and sprinkle with black pepper.

Note If you are unable to find paccheri or giant paccheri for this recipe, you may substitute rigatoni.

Useful Kitchen Tools

COOKING PASTA ISN'T DIFFICULT IF YOU HAVE THE RIGHT TOOLS. HERE ARE SOME OF THE ACCESSORIES THAT CAN HELP YOU IN THE KITCHEN.

1. **Pasta Pot** A pot with a built-in strainer, so pasta can be cooked and drained with ease. It can also be used for boiling asparagus and steaming vegetables.

2. **Butter Curler** A small, effective utensil for making decorative curls from a cold block of butter; the resulting form can make even a simple dish of plain pasta more appetizing.

3. **Large Spider Skimmer** Bigger than a normal skimmer, this handy tool can be used to quickly scoop out cooked short pasta when you want to leave the water in the pot to be used again. This tool can also be used for potatoes and other boiled vegetables.

4. **Serving Tongs** Ones with long, ridged ends make it easier to grasp spaghetti when it comes time to serve.

5. **Spaghetti Measure** This helpful utensil has holes that indicate one or two portions of spaghetti, plus a little hook at the end to capture a single piece of spaghetti when you want to test for doneness.

6. **Cheese Plane** This utensil is perfect for cutting shavings of hard and semi-hard cheeses, to be used for garnishing pasta dishes.

7. **Serving Dish** A deep platter, decorated with fish, vegetables, or shellfish, to indicate the type of food being served.

8. **Wooden Serving Dish** An attractive rustic bowl for bringing pasta to the table.

Glossary

Al Dente
Literally, "to the tooth." This term is used to describe pasta, rice, or vegetables when cooked to the point of offering a little resistance when bitten into without being soft and overcooked.

Corn Pasta
Pasta made from corn has a longer cooking time and a slightly sweeter taste than wheat pasta.

Deglaze
A technique used to make a simple sauce from pan juices or drippings. Pour wine, broth, or other liquid into a hot pan and cook to dissolve the brown bits stuck to the pan, stirring with a wooden spoon. From the French *déglacer*.

Dice
Cut the vegetables into 2½ to 3-inch lengths. Cut in half lengthwise and thinly slice, then cut the slices into strips. Bunch the strips together evenly and cut into ¼-inch cubes.

Julienne
Cut the vegetables into 2½ to 3-inch lengths. Slice each piece in half lengthwise. Place the vegetables, cut side down, on the cutting board. Cut lengthwise into very thin, even slices, then cut the slices into thin strips. For greater regularity in slicing, use a mandoline with a julienne attachment.

Lemon Thyme
Similar to common thyme but with a delicate flavor and citrus fragrance and the same antiseptic and antibiotic properties as common thyme. Used to flavor salads and vegetable dishes.

Mirepoix
A fine dice of onion, carrot, and celery, usually equal parts of onion and carrot and half as much celery. The carrot and celery are sautéed in butter or oil, and the onion is added after a few minutes. The mirepoix should cook until softened and beginning to color. Mirepoix is the base of many recipes.

Mounting
A finishing technique which makes a dish creamy by stirring in butter, cheese, or cream in the last few minutes of cooking. May also refer to finishing gelato.

Pasta Cutter
For cutting fresh pasta dough or pastry. Rolling cutters can have one or more wheels. Multi-wheeled cutters can be regulated and serve to make uniform strips of pasta.

Roux
A mix of butter and flour, often used to thicken sauces, and the base for béchamel. Melt ½ cup (4½ ounces) butter in a saucepan, then stir in 1 cup plus 3 tablespoons all-purpose flour with a spatula. Depending on how long the roux is then cooked, it will be white, golden, or brown.

Simmer
The phase of cooking before a liquid boils. Irregular, tiny bubbles rise to the surface when water or liquid is at a simmer. A delicate cooking technique that lengthens the cooking time.

Turmeric
Herbaceous plant of Asian origin. The root is used to make a bright yellow spice, similar to saffron. It has a slightly bitter flavor, and is one of the ingredients in curry.

Index

A

Anelli with Clams, Potatoes, and Tomatoes, *42*
Anelli with Eggplant and Tomatoes, *54*

B

Baked Ziti with Tomatoes and Provolone, *122*
Black Tagliolini with Baby Squid and Artichokes, *82*
Bucatini all'Amatriciana with Balsamic Vinegar, *132*
Bucatini Nests with Spicy Calamari, *126*

C

Campanelle with Peppers and Escarole, *50*
Casarecce with Clams and Zucchini, *66*
Cavatappi with Morels, Pecorino, and Nutmeg, *68*
Cavatappi with Artichokes, Shellfish, and Tomatoes, *20*
Cold Tortiglioni with Peas and Roasted Peppers, *36*
Corn Fusilli with Shiitake and Porcini Mushrooms, *52*
Corn Tagliatelle with Porcini, Swordfish, and Thyme, *90*
Corn Tagliatelle with Shrimp and Zucchini, *102*

E

Egg Fusilli with Vegetables, *18*

F

Farro Spaghetti with Cauliflower and Olives, *84*
Farro Tagliatelle with Spring Onions and Asparagus, *104*
Fettuccine with Ricotta-Lime Sauce and Turbot, *86*
Fusilli with Radicchio, Artichokes, and Speck, *62*

G

Giant Paccheri with Fish, *24*
Gnocchi with Speck, Peas, and Feta, *58*

L

Ligurian-Style Rice Sedanini, *44*
Linguine with Cherry Tomatoes, Raisins, and Pine Nuts, *112*
Linguine with Octopus and Artichokes, *114*
Linguine with Shellfish, *116*
Linguine with Walnuts and Arugula, *76*

M

Mezze Maniche with Sea Urchin and Peas, *136*

P

Paccheri with Cuttlefish,
 Squid, and Sausage, *130*
Paccheri with Langoustines
 and Eggplant, *28*
Paccheri with Three Peppers
 in White Sauce, *46*
Pappardelle with Vegetable Ragù, *78*
Pasta Nests with Squash Blossoms
 and Baby Squid, *88*
Pasta with Radish Sprouts,
 Broccoli, and Artichokes, *48*
Penne with Green-Bean Pesto
 and Pine Nuts, *26*

R

Radiatori with Zucchini, Anchovies,
 and Arugula, *32*
Rotelle with Fresh Tomato Sauce, *64*
Rotelle with Peppers, Ricotta, and Argula, *56*

S

Saffron Farfalle with Asparagus, *22*
Sardinian Gnocchi with Peas,
 Speck, and Saffron, *70*
Shells with Peas and Carrots, *38*
Shells with Porcini
 and Squash Blossoms, *34*
Spaghetti alla Chitarra
 with Swordfish Ragù, *108*
Spaghetti Nests with Asparagus
 and Chinese Cabbage, *100*
Spaghetti with Clams and Cuttlefish, *98*
Spaghetti with Garlic, Oil,
 and Chili Pepper, *74*
Spaghetti with Shrimp and Green Beans, *110*
Spaghetti with Soft-Shell Crabs, *134*
Spaghetti with Squash Blossoms
 and Squid, *94*
Spaghettini with Broccoli Cream
 and Tuna, *120*
Spaghettoni with Tomatoes, Anchovies,
 and Capers, *106*
Spicy Penne, *40*
Strozzapreti with Calabrian Pesto, *30*

T

Tagliatelline with Zucchini, and Shrimp, *124*
Tagliolini with Scallops, Lentils,
 and Lime, *92*

V

Vermicelli with Clams, 118
Vermicelli with Potatoes and Parsley, 96
Vermicelli with Tuna
 and Tomato Sauce, 80

W

Whole-Wheat Shells with Creamy
 Peppers, 60

Printed in China in September 2008